Falling into Harmony

Falling into Harmony

Memorial Edition

Robin McCorquodale
Et Mortua Est in MMXIV

Copyright © 2014 Robin McCorquodale
All Rights Reserved

ISBN: 978-0-9888632-6-2
Library of Congress Control Number: 2014949418
Cover art: Thomas Moran, "Waterfall in Yosemite"

Manufactured in the United States

Ink Brush Press
Dallas

For William Guest

Poetry from Ink Brush Press

Alan Birkelbach and Karla Morton, *No End of Vision: Texas as Seen by Two Laureates*
David Bowles, *Shattering and Bricolage*
Jerry Bradley, *The Importance of Elsewhere*
Dede Fox, *Postcards Home*
Alan Gann, *Adventures of the Clumsy Juggler*
Jim McGarrah, *Breakfast at Denny's*
J. Pittman McGehee, *Growing Down*
Millard Dunn, *Places We Could Never Find Alone*
Chris Ellery, *The Big Mosque of Mercy*
Charles Inge, *Brazos View*
Steven Schroeder, *a dim sum of the day before*
Steven Schroeder and Sou Vai Keng, *a guest giving way like ice melting*
Jan Seale, *Nape*
Jan Seale, *The Wonder Is*
W.K. Stratton. *Dreaming Sam Peckinpah*
Chuck Taylor, *At the Heart*
Jesse Waters, *Human Resources*
Yarbrough, Scott, *A Sort of Adam Infant Dropped: True Myths*

For information on these and other Ink Brush Press books go to
www.inkbrushpress.com

Introduction

Robin McCorquodale is a writer of genius.

My first peek at her poetry was several years ago when she and I first began working at editing her poems. I clearly recall my amazement at her lively eye for physical detail and her talent for figurative imagery that is unique and musical.

Even though a long-time lover of poetry, Robin experienced such early success as a fiction writer that she was swayed from her original goal of an MFA in poetry to an MFA in fiction. For those of us who love reading and writing poetry, that's a great sadness. As you read these poems, see if you also don't mourn all the additional poems that Robin could have given us sooner.

Not surprisingly, like many other fiction writers who later turn to poetry writing, Robin had to learn to pare down the amount of narrative that a poem might hold. When you read such poems as "Requiem," "Austin Last Night," and "Dal and Doc," you'll see her deft success.

As you linger with these poems, you'll also get a sense of Robin's finely honed gift of crafting the erotic into lines of sophisticated and unexpected power and sheer brilliance. In fact, wherever Robin, as poet, turns her eye she finds a world awash in color and texture which she then hands to us inside the basket woven by her surprising, resonant imagery. In Robin's hands, the entire earth is a precious bauble of heart-breaking beauty and many-headed meaning.

As a fellow multi-generational Texan, I find it pleasing that Robin, as poet, doesn't always look to exotic locales for her poems. You will find poems set in France and New York—both places where Robin lived—but the majority of the poems are set in Texas—on family land, along the Gulf Coast, or in neighborhoods of Houston. So, in her remarkable way, Robin follows that grand old man of American letters, Walt Whitman, in looking around and looking closely at what is contained in the quotidian American life.

Robin's work also gives us a sense of her abundant imagination, particularly in those poems which create historical narrators, such as "The Equestrian Soldier" and "Alcibiades' Mare." One senses this same glorious imagination at work in the many varied "conversations" with artists or other writers in poems such as "Bernini in the Piazza Navona," "Orozco in the Government Palace," and "Typhoon."

Let the brilliant light of Robin McCorquodale's "yellow of a morning/ and orange of an afternoon" bring you to your reading chair. Open her book. Tell your someone special to stay close at hand. These poems are going to flood you with colors of unabashed beauty and remind you how a lover's arms and body can spin you until your heart is full.

And, then...and then, in Robin's own words: "stars/like Royal typewriters will start clicking/on night's black ribbon."

Requiescat in pace.

Sarah Cortez
Houston, Texas

CONTENTS

vii	Introduction by Sarah Cortez
1	Poem from a Basement
3	The Big Thicket
5	Unsolved Crimes
7	Austin Last Night
9	The Turning
10	Two Cats on a Morning Walk
11	Driving Past the Old House
13	Sisters at Jan Austen's Cottage
14	Letter to Kenya
16	Typhoon
19	Grand Opera
21	The Equestrian Soldier
23	When Like a Cloud Bank
24	Alcibiades' Mare
25	Travels with a Drowned Woman
26	Painting Little Black Sambo's Tigers
28	Puzzle Pieces
30	Orozco in the Government Palace
32	Jeanna and I
34	When the Poet Borges Encounters the Deaf
35	Luis Borges the Character of Unreality
37	That Summer Night
39	Questions
40	The Loss of a Comely Man
42	Loving Her
45	Do it in Tempera
46	Nancy and I
48	The Candle beside Me as I Read
49	Preparing Christmas Dinner
51	Dietrich Bonheoffer in My Studio
52	Miss Austen and Charles Baudelaire
54	Rib of a Sundial
55	Sketches
56	Nine-Eleven
58	To Leave a Garden

61	Dal and Doc
64	Wanting You: *Eure-et-Loire*
66	Memory and Mother Goose
69	The Last Monarch
71	Natural Selections
72	The Lover
74	The House this October
76	Baby and Becky
78	Return to Mayan Hegemony
80	A Rocky Road
82	One Gerbera
83	Central Texas 1830
85	Hurricane Ike
86	Waiting for My Second Child
87	The Thirteenth Floor
89	Bernini and the Piazza Navona
91	Requiem
93	Love
95	Superstition
97	Dad and the Kingfisher
99	The French Lover
101	King Lion II
103	William
105	Spindle Piece
106	Sharp Edges
108	The French Hare
109	French Landscapes
111	Mount Sinai

Poem from a Basement

This spring I stayed away
from the Botanic Gardens
and missed the flowering
of the cherries you
gave me cherry cokes
to keep me here
I, who should have
danced Coppelia
and the swan girl
stick by you
spend opening nights
pulling toffee
and testing divinity
I, who should have been
the Queen of Diamonds
snap ginger
wash down
with Royal Crown
I a basement Venus
scratching recognition
from other dancers on point,
cruising the block, and you say,
keep your fingers
off the window bars
your hands out of the street

this fall I stayed away
from Central Park,
was not there to feel
snowflakes on my face;
you gave me almond brittle
to keep me here
massaged muscles
I did not know I had

you brought hissing colas
opened one for yourself
I accepted caresses,
participate in programs
of your choice at 5, 8,
and then again at 10.

Buddha style I sit on a gurney
painting my toenails gold,
while vagrants peer
into the window
believing our apartment
is a chapel.

Circling a cardboard spool
you spin sugar
press it to my lips
watch it melt
then tell me to lie down
midnight you dim the light
at 6 you say the head
has crowned when he is free,
you hold him
by the ankles until he cries
I take him, kiss his cheeks
and each fragile shoulder

on East 13th as my toe-shoes tap
the sidewalk you tell me
this is a stage on which the 3 of us
will dance
collect all 30 phases
of the moon and the snapping stars
our baby looking up at us
feeling the beats.

The Big Thicket

You told me you loved the pine trees,
yaupon berries took your breath away.
Chest to rosined bark, you shinnied
up a pine's stout mast,
made eco prophesies
from an owl's splintery nest,
called the view from there
virgin to your experience.

I sat on your knees,
you plaited my hair
into yellow braids, carved a lyre
from jungle vines, strummed
it into the bright circumference
of our green convictions.
Then you left for California.

I am in the Big Thicket,
shelling a magnolia's thorny cone,
prepared to midwife its seeds' red birth.
I slash through airtight jungles,
gathering blackberries,
enticing a dark-eyed Junco
with a skirt-full.
It eats,
asks my intent,
respects my silence.

Fifty yards off Highway 45,
I stroke the hairy legs
of a brown recluse,
tap its creamy thorax,
smile and gaze into its six eyes.
I carve ladles, hollow out ritual bowls.

Mornings, when dawn pushes
her raspberry tines
across the plot of garden
you made for me,
I fashion a fetish figure,
lick its lips, stroke its hair to bring you here.

Yet from the snowy peak
of Mount Shasta, using its glare
for a light, you write
that all between there
and the redwood forests
is paradise. Are you lying
or do you just love everything?

Unsolved Crimes

The wolves ran out of the shoot,
the pack took a shortcut through a litter
of Albanian gorse, and a young stud coyote
made it past the Cryboy's sheepdog
and jumped the lead Nanny. Tarquinius,
drunk and eager, entered Collatinus' villa at a trot.
Neoptolemus handled Andromache
with the back of his hand. In a Memphis alleyway,
a Union corporal had his way with the actress,
Phoebe Peale, while beside a buckboard
near Vicksburg, six rounds of stragglers fussed
over a startled heifer,
and mules, moiling shyly
in the sticker bushes, broke wind.

Lookie there,
in 800 B.C.E., three walls of a Mayan
religious community collapsed,
at the same time that the dam
Professor Matt Boden
discovered near Merida
buckled and fell. In 1903, the Carmen bros.
ruptured six hymens in a burned-out
Sunday-house in Fredericksburg,
and it's well known that the Roman legion
overstayed its welcome
with the pharaoh's girls. But, hey,
even Romulus bribed a eunuch,
Alexander captured identical twin sisters
drinking from a bucket dipped
in the headwaters of the Euphrates. Maria,
a Barcelonan waitress, made the best
of a bad situation on a butcher block,
while the opal eyes of Polish girls

placed in houses of assignation shattered
like sterile test tubes fallen.
Europa had a wet ride and no choice,
nor did seven women taken last evening in Lagos.
Peggy Simons, chairwoman of the board of NCFC,
caught in March on the mountainous
Chinese border to Nepal, wished she'd done
as the tour guide suggested, and returned
to the hotel with the tour bus.

Whatever happens, daughters of the tribe,
the fox with his superior brush, claws to be first,
and ragged hounds beget bald pups.
In Sudan, teenage boys tied the infirm
and antique to trees. In Ft. Worth,
a member of The Corps violated
Young-Widow-Brown, walking home
from a rerun of *The Sound of Music*
In Congo, ruffians entered a gym
filled with the ninth-grade basketball team;
only 23 percent of the girls cried.

Austin Last Night

Out the screen door,
bats blind as Homer
cut the air with gray tales
and Lear loses a pair of headlights.
When in her crib, Dana raises a fist
and howls, I stagger up my parents' stairs
loosening my blouse. Wind and pods
of rain trees neither rattle nor flap,
leaves refuse to shine either-or
in the moon's cold margins,
and I, like a jagged icicle,
hang from a gutter as my once more-
than-adequate-shape, drips away,
the whole scene worse than this morning
when the Honda of my Prelude
refused to turn right on Deep Eddy
to select an affordable hearse.

See that beside the fountain, Mother sinks
to her knees; her heart loses an entire chamber;
the chimney searches for its missing bricks;
window panes pop out like corn at the movies;
the cocker, Judy, wipes her eyes
on the curls of their paws,
and Toby, the tom, cuffs a wing-broke
sparrow into the black-smoke path
of a leaf-blower made in China.

Members of the clan,
it's not a fuse.
Shut the fuse-box hard,
then enter out of darkness into peace;
accept that the family's dismemberment
rests neither with a fuse

nor the thickening profile of Sagittarius:
Last night my father died.

The Turning

The Brazos River comes to us under a wooden bridge,
a swaying trestle. Petals fall to a black
and yellow blanket. You deal them like cards,
give me half, and we play.
Then we lie, half-sit, elbows for support,
offering each other rabbit pate, gherkins,
and a mustard called Dijon. Slip your foot
under the sand, your hand into the river's pool,
your rump into the spring.
No one will see.
Or what if we put our feet in the water,
let that flirt of a minnow suck 2 decades of toes?
Should we pluck a guinea, share the dark meat
on its thighs? Suppose you kiss my mouth,
slip your hand into my shirt? Imagine
we go halves again and invite the breezes,
thunder, and washboard recitatives
of male crickets. Two squirrels clatter
head to tail, break-neck over the tack-house's
grooved tin roof. Share that sound. Put
a bare leg over this vacation,
your loose hand pulled downstream, your
napping face in sunset's orange shade.
And what if we mix river scents
with the monograms on slips of goose-down
pillows, the cursive R for me, the B for you?
Suppose you ask me to rock you in my arms,
let you tell me again your life-story; identify
the juncture when our dreams became the same?
No, I think I'll play Godiva, dressed this spring
in your redbud's burning limbs.

Two Cats On Our Morning Walk

We're too happy, time the thoroughbred
wins the Jockey Club's Gold Cup
and Dali's watch melts. On Salisbury Street,
behind wrought-iron six-feet-tall, two cats
stare like votive candles lit by a 7:20 sun,
while my fingers play the fence's cool black bars
like harp strings. Neither cat blinks, but we sense
that their music boxes have begun to purr.
See that the black stretches out its hind legs
and the tabby wears for sunglasses
Monet's blue shade.

You call, Kitty; I call, Kitty. The black stays put,
the tabby moves toward us shoulders hunched
like a lioness at a Dallas cocktail party.
We don't know the cats' names,
but we know by their need to start
the day early that we four walk the same
obsessive tightrope. I pitch a pine cone
over the fence; the black rolls it from one paw
to the other and I nod my approval at this
and at the rapid fattening of grazing clouds.
As spicy as nip, your hand takes mine.
You recite from Shakespeare's
Anthony and Cleopatra,
your blond profile like Leslie Howard's
as Ashley Wilkes
I mention S.G.Collette's novella,
La Chatte
and we stroll.

Driving Past the Old House

Last April, that cruel month, I sold my house,
accepted an offer made by a girl child
in her 30s. See my ageratum hedge ripped up,
plants screaming like tortured men
in Maracaibo jails, crows circling
a street dumpster, crying over a lantana sliced,
broken, and pitched. What did it look like,
babes of mine-hers, the descent
of the Spartan's sole?

Above the church steeple
clouds with distended bellies
sprinkle me cold. I run for the house,
reach into my jeans for the key
I no longer have. I rap on the door,
try the bell. My old house is empty, no breath to it.
In daydream interruptions I walk my oak floors
climb the stairs to echoing rooms stroke doors
that look like tongues still tied to mine.

I back up my car, crunch gravel
And take a new way home, the street
covered by branches, leaves slipping together
perfect fits. The garage door slides down.
I rest my forehead against the steering wheel,
knowing later that from my balcony, stars
like Royal typewriters will start clicking
on night's black ribbon; know that it's quits
for screech owls and pine warblers
now absent from the land
I once claimed as my own.
or they, lying in a waste dump,
get used to the truth
of my apostasy,

all of us failing,
I the first to move on.

Sisters at Jane Austen's Cottage

The sun behind a copper beach frowns its shade
near the tree's splayed feet and wrinkled ankles
then begs a thank-you for drying the rain
from the cottage steps, each stone step foot-worn
at its center. Postcards,
black and white photographs of roses,
blue glitter surrounding each. Then
Miss Austen's examples of needlework
presented on a dark table, its surface
with a wide tan scratch.
I tell my sister, Nancy, it's all right to pick them up.
Chawton Cottage, we say, reminds us
of our childhood dollhouse,
rooms so little and so cold.

Northanger Abbey, smaller than my copy
at home, settles in Nancy's hands. She reads
a short passage aloud. We climb the narrow steps
and enter the bedroom where Jane wrote *Emma*.
The desk is small and frail in the legs
as Jane must have been in January of 1817.
Bed covers are eyelet, a single window
gives onto a meadow. We talk of Jane's
genius and craft. Soon a voice from downstairs
says the cottage is closing.

The stairway is dark. Halfway down, I miss a step.
Nancy grabs my arm and we smile.
As the cottage door shuts we hear the lock
grind into place. Nancy's glasses reflect
the sisters' garden. Then she, crying like Cassandra,
grieving, bends to sniff Jane's favorite dark red rose.

Letter to Kenya

This note is not of my wish
but that I've been told by a glass harp
in Jones Hall that there will be something
in writing in the brass mouth
from which your letters once fell
to my Tabriz, but where now
travel brochures stack up as Gulf Coast
storms sore in their sheets level royal palms
and push live oaks into unmanageable floods.

Sweet, I hope to sell our romance,
and though I do not expect much pay,
the sum may serve to buy the plane ticket
I wrote you about, and the train on which I'll ride
to Lake Nakuru, a Pullman for sitting in velvet seats
with brass buttons, not dusty dull like my mailbox
and your former favorite parts of me. You know
I speak truth, and it's not news to you that I wish
for a berth to share with an exotic animal
whom I hope to heaven remains my own.

What I want to say, is that dawn, rising
on a blue-shade park, catty-cornered
from my home, is climbing out vagrant
in orange and falling to the sidewalk
on its rested knees, so to watch the space
filling up with children as my complaint bends
morning's ear to a dirge on the lack of messages.
My housekeeper says that to settle my mind

I should name each red-tailed hawk for you,
each woodpecker, the same– say that cardinals
rattle the firethorns, then eat the blueberries
of everyone's private abacus, arranging

nighttime for 14 hours, training cardinals
to cheep where telegrams once buzzed,
and the fog at the end of a pier
in Mombasa kissed my face and yours.

So I rush to you in writing
and finish this letter like fall days
end sad on their flaps to seal,
though I no longer have your address
and haven't seen you for so long,
among the spiraling seasons, I forget
your stature and the length
of your suntanned legs, though rest assured
I keep your slippers in a shoe box
possessed of the scent of male leather,
though I have heard of your marriage
and the details of its consummation,
after which the funeral cortege, complete
with a reliquary of our journal-of-days
in a Cornell box, among dry seeds left there
by a lover's dreams on access roads obfuscated
by rainclouds prepared to cry their waters.
I eager to recover the soul you took, snarl
at my mailbox like a hydrophobic dog
that in its incompleteness, can never cease
to rip and bite; its wishing to find,
instead of bruises, a photo of you
in its brass beak, you wandering
in the bush, wishing for a pen and paper
with which to write to me,
as Darcy wrote to Elizabeth
and King Mark to Isolde, you driving
a Jeep Wrangler in the Kenyan outback,
lost, weeping, and alone.

Typhoon

> *To the poet, Kenneth Koch, continuing our*
> *conversation spring of '70*

What I want to say, Kenneth,
is that I was wrong about art
being rational. I thought it was something
harvested from the imagination's
convergences, cotton picked from bolls,
ginned, and sold. Dreams, Kenneth,
except we were awake.

Talent's not enough,
I preached to angry crowds,
wishing to stick my head on a pole
and lead their own parades. Structure's
where it's at, I told the remaining few.
What I mean is I believed art should slip
into Plato's pigeonholes; I thought reflection
stood tall in God's bell curve, merciful,
unlike lightning, which claws black-bottomed
clouds raw; rips them off with the smacks
Jeremiah predicted and for it was snuffed out,
as in a gale curlews, avocets, and herons
hit the fan and the sting of rain pains sea bass
and jellies alike.

Now I anticipate peevish tides engulfing
neophytes and cognoscenti
as if they were blue crabs
made to skate on corrugated roofs
or buzzards off-course, seeking grain
in lieu of carrion, then falling ill of bloat,
as in 1900, a typhoon hit Galveston Island
and removed the 6,000. My point is this:
Every 5 or 6 years, as soon as

A typhoon hops out of the gulf's belly,
as Athena hopped out of Zeus' head,
drive 40 miles to the Gulf Coast,
lean on the hood of a drowned-out pickup;
compose a crop of metaphors, using a beach
strewn with flopping redfish and a two-eyed
bottom fish named Ray. That way,
in a month, you can leave Barnes and Noble
with a Cuban cigar between your teeth
and a copy of *Esquire* under your arm.
That's art, Kenneth, money in your pocket
and the prints of lipstick on your cheeks.

First Communion

at 7 I am in a bride dress
a crown of pansies on my head
white satin ballerinas for my feet
a fingertip veil blowing in the wind
to photograph.
Nana on one side, Nanie on the other,
ink blue silk dresses to their ankles
black lace-up shoes 2-inch heels
Little Princess, they say
as if that were my baptism's tag,
Two grandmothers wanting me for love
but Mother's my love, me wanting her
to hold me at night hear my dreams by day
her asking me to sing Toora loora loora
after she picks me up at school
such a pretty voice
you are my Irish rose.
All right.

then Nana dies and I cry too much in my bed,
and ask past midnight for another doll
Mom hits me bare-butt lying across her knees
5 years later me still dreaming I'm lying in a crib
its sides like window screens to confuse,
malaria, a fever called yellow, and flies;
the top hooked down
so I can't stand up full;
my keeping silent on this one
let my husband
rock me for crying.

Grand Opera

member the weekends you hitchhiked
800 miles from San Diego to Mills College
loving me all week an ensign
diving submarines you writing to me Hegel Jung
and thermodynamics me living days
6am to 9pm with 18th century counterpoint
at 19, years an opera contender too shy to sing
yet crying during the Metropolitan's Saturday
broadcasts of Verdi, Puccini, Donizetti, Bellini
member the weekend of the Berkeley Hills
fettuccini alfredo candle flame smells of pine
jumping up falling back on your dark face
eyes like lightning broadcasting royal blue
German wine fit snug in its straw basket
crunching garlic toast me telling you
I wanted you that night to breach an iconic wall
your teeth grabbing your lip head nodding
swallowing hard us riding 15 minutes
to the Berkeley Hills, handbrake-parked
on a cliff that fearsome first mating
you loving me to death,
never stop loving next year I flew like the bird
I'm named for to the Julliard School
tried my luck and won the ribbon

you and I lost track of where we left off
still we left off now me with HIM
in San Francisco *cara nome* last fall in Seattle
un bel di next spring you with HER
Thanksgiving in Bethesda grandson
maybe in a highchair, you pulling
with him the turkey's last wishbone
your family laughing
high-pitched just a bunch of geese

come to roost in sunset trees you
telling them sea stories all but one
me with my family's wishbones
membering how God in the water
we could make love.

The Equestrian Soldier

Pavilions of silver streak backward
along the Apian Way. Cavalry rides small
under poplars through mists from skies
our lord Hannibal claims for his own. Trails
remain vertical, ice to slip across till dark.
An elephant falls to its knees and bawls,
while I, standing in three-foot snow, drink it
for water; I, who must clean and hone
spear and sword; I, with nothing to anticipate
but a half-hour for lunch and a nap
where I'll force sleep, counting snowflakes
to twelve or twenty. Pain, promises of silver
and a brooch for the neck
of my small brown wife.

>   Hannibal to his brother Hamilcar
>   From the hill above Valladolid:
>   *I led a splendid cavalry advance*
>   *on Nova Carthago. Crossing the Alps*
>   *proved easy. My Algerians fought*
>   *with knives held in their white teeth,*
>   *a spear and a sword in each hand.*
>   *In the Po Valley we moved in formations*
>   *I'll describe as bird-wing.*

Fearful that my pony will fall headfirst
into cracks in stone tables, I lean backward
and think of rolls in the hay with baby,
while boney branches, sweeping my face,
make gashes on which our surgeon will place
a smoking iron. Next day uphill, I hang for agony
onto my horse's frozen mane,
my raw cheek laid open on its neck.

> Hannibal to Hamilcar:
> *At Cannae, I sent cavalry to the Roman*
> *right flank, a surprise maneuver,*
> *yet one the enemy expected. It was thanks*
> *to the fluid movements of the equestrian*
> *soldiers that the plan gelled. Roman*
> *lines broke, the rubbish surrounded.*

Bathing in a hot salt pond, I massage my thighs,
swollen and salted like a pair of Spanish hams.
Let me tell you that when I dismount I am helpless
to put one foot before the other; I'm like a harp
that cannot be plucked for music. We cross
gnarled turf, making our way to giggling brooks
cooled by the goddess Tanit's finest exhalations.

> *Yet it was the equestrian soldiers*
> *who most excelled. One of them,*
> *an orchestra of bravery unto himself,*
> *caught your noble head and with it*
> *under his arm cantered to me.*

My animal whinnies. I limp past the sentinels,
see its hoof caught in a chain cast there by a weary
foot soldier. The groom, Abdul, says, "Unwind
the chain, hang it on that olive tree
where Tuscan stars will light your return to camp."
But that night, the moon, that spur, that goat horn
of a lunar clef, catches in my black hair
and pitches me, rollicking to extinction
four hundred kilometers from Florence,
six hundred years
before Michelangelo's *David*
and Botticelli's
The Birth of Venus.

When Like a Cloud Bank

When like a cloud bank
I, the bride, left the black sky limousine,
gray church stones made a dove of my visage,
while carved Romanesque saints
smiled at the church school.
The cleric greeted me not at all
as Calchas greeted Iphigenia,
and green-cushioned pews
(felled poplars on the Appian Way)
held the families
and friends of us both.

Like a refreshing summer shower
the flower girl ran out of petals
and ran to her mother. Bridesmaids
(satin blush colors apricot to rose)
evoked sunset, dawn, as Fragonard. Watteau
and Boucher's goddesses as they ask to lie
in the lap of Apollo; pink hands touching him
where it counts, otherwise stroking Minou's tummy,
or the back sides of cupids ready for pleasure,
though not for love.

Alcibiades' Mare

Alcibiades, Athenian general, politician,
saved in battle by Socrates, I need you
to rein me in, braid my tail, rub down
my withers, and adjust my halter
so the buckle doesn't scrape my cheek.
I need you to hold me
between your knees.

Conqueror, gentleman,
I know not your name in its entirety,
nor does Volume I of the 1910
Encyclopedia Britannica, but its lyricism
makes an equine's flesh twitch,
and its mind know with certainty
that hawthorn berries and olives
in their time will fall on the road
during our drive into Sparta.

At thirty, you climbed on my back
again at thirty-one. Deceiver, opportunist,
we linked on the island of Naxos,
where from sunset to sunrise we shared
secrets under the torment of debauchery,
frequent possession, no indication of infidelity,
word for word, bark for bark, as puppies raced
round my pasterns, nipping.

Delium, my lord! Cries for the young men's victory,
a pair of teenage girls for each;
pails of grape seeds for me
and a white heron to follow my prints
in the sand, its neck bent to peck seeds
from my shat. Alcibiades, at the sound
of your name my eyes tear.
Say it!

Travels with a Drowned Woman

Your Sunfish topples, you fail
to take hold of the stern. The sail
wraps your thighs, salt water
stings your throat, and your spine,
once as straight as Telemann's oboe,
plays its reed bent out of shape
by barnacles attached to a pier.
while strings of your life preserver
work loose, you so altered
that a man-o-war
draws its ribbon tentacles
to its breast. You beckon to a young shark;
that sniffs your elbow, and retreats
like a prize fighter refusing a match.

Minnows form for you
a veil of secrecy; clams filtering water
open and shut in dull-green voids,
their swinging doors like those in brothels,
the madam wishing to use for gain
the baby daughters
you'll never have.

A random hull scraps your chest,
a snapper furthur shreds your skin,
blue crabs quarrel to make nests
in the seat of your plankton chair.
And shrimpers, on a busman's holiday,
drop their hooks. One catches
in your cheek poor shining shrimp
its head half off, shell broken,
you now in the vortex
of a sudden squall, its pausing
a long moment to chide you
for drowning at not quite 17.

Painting Little Black Sambo's Tigers

Mom, you let me into your studio mornings
yellow blue burnt sienna oils
under my fingernails dashes of pink
on my rain lily cheeks moms charcoal
scratching rag paper me 8 years old
painting tigers gold and black racers
melting into butter for Black Mumbo's
pancakes me hoping to meet that boy
Sambo help him with his words in school
alongside the polio boy who sunned
himself each morning across the street
but we can't talk about Sambo anymore
my book hidden under the attic eaves
a mouse cutting baby teeth ripping the spines
while a roof leak made wavy pages quick to tear.

Then in France May of '40
when Hitler sends in his steel
Sambo 17 at the country club
serving Christmas to gold button
olive drab fly boys dragging
on Raleigh cigs settled in silver cases
like organ pipes Chivas Regal
flowing one frowning says
no ice Sambo. In Tuskegee he earns his wings
the right to fly a fighter P-51 tail painted red
no allied bomber he escorts bursts
into a carnation he at 86 missions
and gaining
then July of '44
15 years after Martin Luther King's birth
and when the army still didn't allow
black nurses to feed a white boy
or arrange his tourniquet

on a battle field and one day
after his best friend gets killed,
Sambo volunteers to fly a cardboard one-engine
over German artillery emplacements
he takes a bullet an angel makes the catch
asks him to describe the best day of his life
he says it was when a girl brought to school
a painting she did as her mom read to her
about me tricking tigers to fast-forward
around a palm tree till they turned to butter,
she and I, and we knew it,
just a couple of cleverer then hell
American kids.

Puzzle Pieces

Imagine two people talking about a ranch 150 miles
from Dada's silver mine. See them at 16,
flinging beer bottles from the boy's pickup.
He lives in a house like *Giant,* she in a trailer park
on the highway to Laquitas. They put together puzzles
of the other's choice,
drink colas from frosted mugs.
Alongside the flooded Rio Grande,
water-soaked leaves hide sidewalks,
clog gutters, block roads in Presidio.
Two people cycling dodge hail near Balmorhea.
The boy kisses the girl; when he slides his hand
under her jacket she shuts her eyes,
and does what only she can do, her pelvis
so able, so attentive, and so kind.

Imagine two puzzle pieces, joined in marriage;
when one sparks like flint, the other yields,
then begs a many times humped up cloud
for cool water. When it delivers, she makes
a pot of iced Lipton to accompany
homemade brownies after church.

At last, when in their garden on College Street
a fountain drops its skirt, and sparrows lay siege
to its lip, two people claim their favorite pieces
of the other and mate.

Imagine an Easter picnic where they tickle and paw,
flex their feet at the egg-white affability of clouds,
and on a May night slip their fingers into the 8th and 9th
of Saturn's rings. On the 4th of July,
they butcher a lamb, light sky-rockets
while their little sons strike matches
to a box of sparklers and spin.

Imagine that when death pushes its dusty shoes
onto the heart of one, the other can no longer
link the puzzle pieces, or change a yawning moon
to alertness; not after this poem
has lost the most colorful pieces in its box.

Orozco in the Government Palace

I take a horse taxi
down your broad streets
occasioned with horse balls
and well-fed roses hanging
on green taped wire stems
a collared monkey
snatching a dollar
for each one I pick then
entertaining me
with pretty somersaults
in the air Orozco
genius painter man of parts
I have picked these fragrant divas
thinking they will complement
your palette and act as foils
for your fascination with chicanery
and machines
see that I make my offering
of rose petals the color of tongues
pinked by shears of dressmakers
with onyx eyes.

José Clemente the saints placed
brush and crayon in your hands
but where did you take the communion
essential to making you purge iniquity
from the stronghold of politics and lust?
I see your offering climb the curved walls
brown workers in blackened factories
lithe Indians with naked legs
opening the arteries of silver mines
dark women wrists bound floating
on their backs in the eternal tides
of the male imagination see how

they sink in drowning waters
like Aztec fish

if there is time will you share with me
your palette's colors
allow me to make copies in the office here
slip them into my satchel
for in my mind's eye i see your sweating seasons
on a scaffold painting penances
on skinless faces exorcized during
yet another theft of power. How many
more arrows of terror will glance off your subjects'
bones exhibited here like the dry thorn forests of Oaxaca
since surely you asked Trotsky
for his blessing in making each man's
ecstasy a sure thing
just look how the young Pueblan
beside me bows before masterpieces
of protest then kneels to press his forehead
to stones on which his father's jailers tread
notice he had risen with eyes and mouth
wide open like men convicted of playing dead.

a horse taxi brought me here
wooden wheels
wobbling on cobblestones
three-legged rabbits
running one after another
between the horses' scarred legs,
yet yellow hibiscus suns
still with blood in their throats
means there has been no resolution at all.

Jeanna and I

The day I loved you most
was Christmas of '43
when I unwrapped a present
a cage and inside a yellow canary
you said could sing
but I didn't think so

or 1949 when you wakened me
with a kiss said that on this day
we had to go to court
I needed to identify
the driver who ran a stop sign
and killed my friend Mary Jane,

or was it in '52 your pride in me
when a senior at Rice
called to ask me for another date
and I was 16
and he loved me.

or in '61 my 1st child
your 4th grandchild
this one a boy who looked
like his dad walked at 10 months
and talked in sentences at 2.

or perhaps '73 on Galveston beach
our eyes the same color
2 blue herons landed on a mirrored cloud
rocking on Galveston's pleated bay
both birds good at fishing
and relaxed about it.

No surely it was '88
2 years before your death
when we painted together
in Brewster County,
silver petticoats of rain sliding
over the Twin Sisters' peaks
our sucking in our breaths
and emitting whispered screams
at the gorgeous art work
on the canvas of the other.

When the Poet Borges Encounters the Deaf

December, 6 o'clock Borges
sits in a plane talking
as if he can see the moon
as it fashions copies of itself
in rotating stone and pins them
to the undersides

of blue winter clouds

as he senses the warmth
of a hostess passing
he says to her I am blind
from childhood
so will you count
the streetlights
below in Houston
and tell me the number of cars

say if we have already passed
the pine forests of East Texas
describe the docking ships
and the refineries flaring
gas candles
soon yet still without answers
he grasps the cuff of her jacket
and tells her that his seat is so small
its arms have bruised his elbows

she reaches into her pocket
for a Marks-A-Lot and writes
the names and conditions
for debarking on the palms
of his youthful hands.

Luis Borges the Character of Unreality

Reader, please allow me
to pet the sun's crisp head,
reply to the squeaking joints
of my old cat, call the vet
rock on my heels let kitty-kitty
suck a sweetened
Nanny goat's pap
is it so impossible to understand
that another cat crouches before a saucer
of broken meat
cats found by me
and nourished
while my lame eyes dart and the works
I create jump like beans knocking
on the high heeled shoes
of Argentine women?

Sightless I cannot tie my shoes
and I Jorge Luis Borges will never see
the French architecture of Buenos Aires
or the diptych of Juan Peron and his Eva
though through a mist
I have mixed reds and blues
to make purple lick alive
the weakest of my verbal expositions.

(softly) Listen to the click-clutch
of my poet's purse; my wish
to voice elation in each verse
so to feel the devil's finger
lift my sex enough I have learned
that a mob's feet run like water
from a washtub's full-out tap why fine weather
here in South America means sunshine

seasoned with anise to cook my straw hat.
Or look here in the square, the ambient air smelling
of his sweat and mine
so that with eyelids shut
and a wave of a magician's baton
I evoke the color black and invite
him then to take my turn careening atop
the 18-wheeler of last night's mare
always watching as I remove my nightcap
and with this arm linked to my woman's.
(whispered) Reader, tell your friends
the vigor of my tropes
as you editor with your tuning fork
slip exactions into the groin
of my thickening guilt. For what human male
does not blanch for his part in childbirth?

Be kind, lay me down beside my cats
place fresh dogwood petals
on the undusted cirrus clouds
I own for eyes. Permit me to dream
again in verse; see that I have learned
to graze in this pair of lame meadows;
my 2 schoolboy blackboards
cracked at last, thunderheads shaking
a genius's cone-shaped berm.
I nervous with hope yet then gone,
my blood blue from repeated beatings.
Dear God, I hear the werewolf panting;
it licks my hand, sees me kneel to the werewolf,
who howls for his dead sons.
I snap the fingers of both hands
whistle between my teeth
Here, boy, and he comes.

That Summer Night

there was a dinner party
on Piney Point Road
the garage decorated in French café,
Lautrec of Toulouse on a wall-size poster
of a full breasted woman dancing
hip bones to hip bones
with a severely skinny man
red and white checkered cloths
a tape playing Piaf throat tones
to break our hearts and then some

when you came in
my wine glass tipped to drink
my lips on the rim, you stalled
in the doorway checking
out the room
eyes like a yacht's searchlights
seeking a well–outfitted port of entry
and they stopped on me
your blond hair bathed by an overhead bulb,
you as electric as a NFL quarterback
hunting down a receiver
sure to make the catch

Who I asked? and my sister N
called you by name.
When the clock in the hallway
rang 9 I with my man for the evening
I took a cigarette from a case
you asked if I needed a light

in 2 steps there at my arm
your warm lighter flared
I bent close, my hand on your wrist

where the fire found the diamond I wore
You engaged?
Not exactly
Six of us remained for a nightcap
you talked of Peru
a year in Lima
then Paris
you a soldier translating
French newspapers
for high command
you preening I smitten
wondering how many more pieces
of gold you were yet to leave
on my feral mind's now besotted table
Monday with difficulty I taught
my 5th graders
at home i paced
the floor watching the squat
black telephone fail to ring.

A week passed home alone
I browsed the book for your number
ran a finger down names beginning
with M

two days after Christmas
enough red poinsettias
to remind us of nature's treasury
white orchids and stephanotis
in my hands as shaken
as white sparrows in a gale
N's little girl dropping rose petals
my English mother crying
an Irish father to give me away.

Questions

It seems I spend my life
waiting for *Swan Lake* to begin,
scenery to turn my eyes
to cones of cherry ice,
my leaping into the arms
of a prince there to catch me,
balance me on his palm,
lower me. I dance pirouettes
on point, one knee bent,
starched crinolines scratching
my thighs and tutu as white
as Pavlova's face.

Only three snow maidens
wait with me. Where are the others?
In their cars locked in traffic,
or in a changing room
angry that the only remaining
rouge color is mauve?
Why so few of us ready to dance
prince and male courtiers
never here at all? What are we
but snow maidens
under a spotlight circling,
without a Nureyev to catch us
or a baby to crawl the floor?

The Loss of a Comely Man

I should have known by the civility
of waves tonguing stanchions
that my day had come; guessed
by blue crabs circling that your arms
extended to me for love meant
you had a baited hook.

I, pray God, should have attached
a white flag to my female rigging,
modified my side-glancing eyes,
painted my nails as green as this Gulf,
then beckoned to you with one of them.

For you, I should have given the oyster bed
of my parts, watched sun-fired hotshots
strike your surging buttocks,
sandy ripples at my back,
my knees cast up
toward pale blue December's
cotton bale sky. with daring moves,
fashioning a veil of salty air,

I should have changed my starfish stares
to ephemeral lightness. Dipping
into a breaker's rising shoulders,
I should have let you service
its kinetic pleasure
and my corporeal one;
you, emerging,
dark hair hauling water,
feeler dangling,
while snarling waves
raced to extinction
on Galveston's creamy slip.

Memory, birth in glossy prints,
I should have accepted
the spray of your lure,
let you sprout in me
a wailing child, two weeks
before Dickens on the Strand.

Loving Her

I do not know
exactly why I love her
why I keep coming back
wherever she is is it because
we were 9 together
in 4th grade us humming
America the Beautiful
while Betty Bernard recited *Breathes
there a man with soul so dead
who never to himself hath said,
"This is my own my native land,"*

or because in school
we were the asthmatics
who in winter couldn't run the bases
or because at 13 we were too shy
to let a boy put his arm around our shoulders
Friday nights in the movie balcony,
or because at 14 we went
to summer camp and rode look-alike
palominos in a rodeo,
and a 16-year-old cowboy,
who rode bulls,
whistled.

back home at a formal dance
our first corsages and 3 years later
my cousin Bobby her date for the prom,
or because at 19 she said
she'd cover for me, say if my father
called I was spending the night with her
when I was in the Rice Hotel letting a man
Dad hated make love to me or because at 22
I married a winner who gave me

three kids and she married a drunk
who vanished when Andrea
was 5 months old or that her mother
died and left her the family home
she couldn't maintain,

or 20 years later Bill and I
found her on her living room floor
soiled, sick, and addled,
and Andrea playing hippy
in Boulder never came.

Fridays I go to see her
she sits in a wheel chair
near the piano away from the others
their singing hymns, missing
90% of the words. Some heads
on chests dozing, wasted arms slack,
pianist and singer bringing
their young voices and Jesus,
her gray hair brushed and combed
blue eyes as bright as when in '68
we went to Naxos
college girls looking
through turquoise water
at the scarlet paint on our 20
impossible-to-tell-apart toes

she strains to sit tall
she cannot till I walk
towards her my arms wide out
like wings of a gull flying
over twinkly waters
of do-you-remembers.
I carrying grabbed-by-the-neck gladiolas
hurry to her my heart holding its beats
then I, taking a leap,

she and I mixing our ripples
to blend just as we did that afternoon
when in a 4th grade classroom
(Mom and Mother sitting in back)
a spotlight parallelogram of sun
marking our stage as we hummed
America the Beautiful
Betty B. reciting Walter Scott at 9.

Do It in Tempera

The back of a seemly photographer,
a photo of him in wader's trunks;
short-billed dowitchers, color prints,
Louisiana herons, sandpipers, white ibis;
beach pictures of the Gulf of Mexico.
Click! great white herons without canes;
marbled godwits rolling on wheels.
Click that pair!
Pelicans playing kamikaze, a picture
of avocets resting, overlapping prints,
sea gulls writing in Sanskrit
with Mandarin pens, lily whitecaps
outrunning silver moons;
a porpoise couple rising
to bark and breathe; Winslow Homer's
horsehair brush, seaweed bearding
a gray dog's mouth, black Nikons
exposed in public. What we know,
tritons are mermen. Find that album.

And jelly fish grow young again.
Click a picture of that growth;
that a female barracuda serves 12 for dinner;
that those sand sculptures up yonder, rival
Niki de Saint Phalle, Bernini, Donatello, and Rodin;
that yards of switch grass clothe naked dunes;
stretched cirrus clouds cry water for gouache;
stone-hard ripples in sand make kinetic corrugations;
the eyes of red snappers at Gaido's Seafood tear;
sand cranes, like teenage boys, need no stilts.
That James Audubon obsessed on water fowl.
Click!
Or separate an egg, honey, beat the yolks.
Do your artwork in tempera,
make them last a thousand years.

Nancy and I

Trinity Bay, the breeze
sang deep Melchior, then dried
by the black-night manes
of strolling ponies,
put us children to sleep.

A windmill loose on its core
labored and creaked. Summer roses
shut their eyes and unfolded petals
to reveal breasts of interest to August's
lascivious eye, while September mentioned
to faded irises that the subject
of their prayers should be
to receive paint of a brighter color.

Beside us on the porch swing,
Nanie told stories that turtles
and newts heard from the rice canal;
and cows heard as they shifted places
among the corn stalks gone deaf
from missing ears. Then we
and Nanie's princes grew brave
and strong and married.

Low of Aberdeen Angus, snakes
slithering up conjugal skirts, willfully
unhindered and blessed by a priest,
while breezes combing salt grass, thrilled
our petted bodies, our flowered heads
and theirs resting silky
as Mayday ribbons on matching
goose feather pillows,
all of this supported
by out-of-the-bedroom-window

streamers of our imaginations,
as wind from the southeast,
touches our limbs and faces
and those of pear trees budded.

God as poised for action
and at attention as a favorite host
could ever hope to be, he arranging
for the universe to fall into a harmony
of pieces, filling the sky
with the exotic stars
we call our children.

The Candle Beside Me as I Read

Ten o'clock. I blow hard
on a flaming candlewick.
A white string of smoke
makes a chimney
of my lampshade,
and from my reading chair
and hassock, I glance at the ceiling,
then into the 4 corners of the room.

Where did the wispy cloud go?
Why has something so beautiful
left my room?
I shut the window,
light the candle,
blow it out easy
ah, there.

Preparing Christmas Dinner

I don't know what to do with December,
when blue chills color Taurus Minor,
planets playing jacks lose their balls
calling them moons; you and I standing
so close our features blur.
See that my eyes melt into yours
like ice blocks stacked near a field of burning timber.
How inimitable we feel sunk deep in our mattress,
while the movie channel at the foot
of our king bed presents, as if a new flick,
Gone with the Wind, where Rhett marries Melanie
who doesn't die. Or Shane, and Marian is widowed.

Yesterday, from your balcony we observed neighbors
arriving home, and so, for their amusement,
we climbed down a network of clotted rose vines
to mine. Note that I taped strings
of Christmas lights on each stone parapet,
then waited till you seized the day,
kissed me ragged, till we hung ravaged
by each color that sunset offered.
As for the petal pinks and blood oranges,
we stored them in our Steinway's bench.
You complementing with yours my mouth's insistence.

What are we thinking now in the kitchen,
as soft in our heads as teddies? Answer
while I push garlic cloves under this lamb
leg's skin and like a surgeon sew up the sides
where the bone once lay. Put your hands
at my waist, then trust them to slip
around your favorite parts of me. Rest your chin
on my head, cup the sisters of my breasts
lick the nipples softly each in its turn.

Then tell me how soon
we shall fall over the familiar cliff,
and along with sunset's Gallic glow
and night's Celtic pot shots, share a bottle
of Russian River red and brag
of our unique ascensions.

Dietrich Bonheoffer in my Studio

The day I laid my forehead
against my writing table
and cried, I'd been distracted
by a bit of yellow tablet tacked
under the light switch
where I had written a line
about the arc of history
being long, but curving
toward justice. Strange,
I couldn't remember
having written that.
I glanced out a window
half the size of my studio's
north wall at a gathering
of sparrows, pecking
among the flagstones.
I asked Mr. Bonheoffer,
must they or I implement justice,
my knee smashed,
my man's tendon cut,
our dead baby?

Miss Austen and Charles Baudelaire

I call Central Texas to see how you are.
You won't talk about it;
we segue to Jane Austen's *Emma*.
Mr. Knightly is too old for her
you say I ask you not to spend nights alone;
tell the nurse-sitter to stay You say Emma
is a busy body. I agree. Thursday
you tumble down 3 steps, hit your head
on the bronze image of Dad's pointer Belle
Dr. K telephones from Seton's trauma
If we don't operate
M and I drive 160 miles
three hours later
surgery's a success you asleep
like a Fragonard nymph
except for plastic tubes in your nose.
Dr K. smiles and I do; M lies full-out
on a sofa in the waiting room
lips moving along Beaudelaire's
Le Balcon. We drive up the hill
to Red Bud Trail large oil paintings
of yours on every wall and in the fridge
smoked chicken and a crumbly
wedge of chevre. Half past midnight
the phone rings we hurry
in the dark of the morning coffee
in thick-lipped U.T. mugs
we ask to see you your eyes closed,
feet dressed in racy plum socks knobs
on the soles to keep from slipping
green-blue eyes if they would just open
in an 8x10 office, Dr. K switches on a light
behind a picture, points to a hemorrhage.
She'll be helpless

movement in only one arm
I telephone Menlo Park Santa Cruz
and Seattle. Sibs say do it
and we do. It's raining,
windshield wipers
ticky-tock ticky-tock
We move around your home in Christmas robes
silent except for my weeps and M's hugs
and I'm sorrys. Piled against the barbecue shed
he finds logs flames leap past the open flue
we sit on the hearth holding hot chili in Lenox bowls;

ten days later, 5 o'clock Houston-time,
an urn of ashes crushes 8-year-old star lilies
you laid across Dad's coffin.
As we leave the family plot a dark man
in overalls begins filling the trench.
I go back, ask him for the spade
but I cry too much and must return it.
In the car its motor running
M watches me his wrist
bent over the steering wheel
I ask him if he'll go with me to the cathedral
in Winchester and visit Jane's grave.
He will.
I ask him if he's hungry

we drive to Ninfa's on Navigation
and M, his face composed, eyes flinty
with light, shares with me a margarita
and the Baudelaire.

Rib of a Sundial

The yellow of a morning
and orange of an afternoon
strike sundials. These lights
need never change,
though some of us,
as we screw a gray bulb
into a socket pretend it does. Lucy,
our American
shorthair, pretends to like dry food,
though it clogs her teeth
and flattens her mezzo mew.
Songbirds pretend
to enjoy cold mornings, though frost
irritates small hearts.
I pretend that you love me,
though you stand at attention
and salute any flag in any parade
at all. Yet I know you like me next to you;
the fleetness of your steps toward me
as I feign sleep impose a shadow
that tells me so, and I hear: It's time,
or Robbie, your time has come,
indicating dawn's possession rather
than midnight's struggle to arouse
vacant sundials, as when you waken
and slide your hand to the pinnacle of my nest,
and arrange the salient best of you to probe
the innards of the fleshiest of poems,
and leave them heavy with child.

Sketches

    1.

A camellia the color of sunrise
bursts its bud wide open
who cares if it doesn't last longer
than a few hours
floating in a fish bowl
that lost its last fish
a decade ago?

    2.

Quiet the moon
like my baby's
sleeping face ;
its spotlighting a gesture to me
a breeze a ripple then another
in the moon boy's catch
sliding the tip of a water-nipple
into its mouth pursed
as always for a kiss.

    3.

Jacket stained with blood
and stuck with cockleburs,
my brother streaks out of the woods
to claim lunch. Bow in hand,
five arrows missing from his quiver of 12
he circles the house, red towel
floating behind him eyes squinting
to hold 12-noon's blind violence;
he, 7 years old, 6 hours after dawn
catches the sky's breath and with it

picks, he says, a willing
rose named Sharon
and brings it to me.

Nine-Eleven

Let it be a fait-fixe that only when the sun shines
can we see our shadows and know who we are.
That this morning, a pair of planes
made Whitman's Mannahatta smoke;
made the terrier you walked last night
lose its bark; made flamed ashes sting
like hornets, and surgeons to arrive too late
to break the knees of the three thousand.

Know that blue is black, that pythons
constrict lions and cats alike;
lily pads wilt in flowing gutters
their faces robbed of green;
angel fish turn belly-up in Zuni bowls,
patterned with lighting;
that the infant you rocked
last evening bleeds from its rose,
and we, our backs bent like harp frames,
lose our way to St. Vincent's,
and cannot find Father,
or the Arthur Miller-boy, Biff.

Know that geese quilt the sky we used to call
Gainsborough's *Blue Boy*, then spin
like footballs into the hands of wide receivers
to whom we've not been introduced. Understand
that Cain has refused to apologize to his parents;
Noah has refused small animals passage
on the arc; that Seth has murdered
the gentle Horus; and that the young man, Ham,
has looked again on the nakedness of his dad.

To Leave a Garden

I don't like to leave our garden
and fly to France, sage blossoms,
purple fires in the middle ages,
which once, you said, on the way to Alba,
restored to heaven the broken bodies
of heretics in Albigensia.
My ticket says Wednesday,
an aisle seat for which an airline
employee scrambled. And there's
the question of what to pack. And should
I take the speed-train to Marseilles,
a side-trip to Grasse? Will five
in the afternoon at the Tuilleries,
my return outdoors from hardwired
rooms of the Louvre, go unnoticed?
Will plane trees cast
shadows on my sunhat and the toes
of my pumps? May I hope to buy
a mushroom crepe from the green awning
wagon at la Place de la Concorde?
Will undersized cars spin like the blades
of Cleopatra's fan, cars dragging sunny sheets
through brassy autumn slide into the fountain?
Will someone filch my passport
in a swaying metro car between Concorde
and La Porte Maillot? Will crepes, baited
with rosemary and a laurel leaf taste good?
Pity me, since our cycling tour in Burgundy,
I cannot find my adapter; though I told you
about this on a ride from Dijon to Beaune,
ideas and plans, racing on the silky tracks
of our minds as a 2-year-old Arabian racer
is pursuing a dyspeptic fox?

And, Cheri, what about Henri II
and Diane de Potier
and Henri II's untimely death,
or Philip the Bold?
over a glass of Clos Vuguet?

You're gone, begonias rock
your memorial in bird nest baskets
where I hooked them to the gutter.
Will tiny dinosaurs congregate
in monkey-grass borders, and grouse
about my absence? Do they, as I,
beg you to return? Do their beds
feel as chilled and cloudy as Paris
Februarys pushed up from Le Havre?
While I'm gone, will composts
refuse to rot, or compass points swing
as they should? Will the fountain's pool
turn green; grains of plant-food harden
in the box? How about my suitcase filled,
yet still open on the luggage rack? I stick
my nose into a rain lily's calyx;
the flower blushes and I,
who have pitched my tent for a year
in this garden among rhomboid leaves
attracting heady clouds to act as buttresses
to brace what's left of me. Mark you,
this garden
and its subjects, I and our sons
still stroll among your blue and gold
petals, while squirrels crack pecans
and stare with black-fig eyes
into the space in which we last saw you,
cleaning your racing bike,
then slumped upon a slender tire,
drops of oil on your Viking-fair cheeks.
From this garden, you sucked past

telephone poles and the broad
faces of magnolias; this event
that doubtless drew to you a clique
containing Charlemagne, Roland,
Le Conde, and the obsessive Corsican,
call me now to our French brothers,
13 years after you and I left Paris.

Dal and Doc

when I was 7, 8, and 9, I rode
on calls with my grandfather Dal.
Smells of ether rubbing alcohol
pig leather of Dal's doctor bag; Dal
the surgeon, letting me put
his stethoscope in my ears
and listen to his busy heart.
Doc the collie in the back seat
face outside the window
sorry for dogs running the fences
barking, not invited to ride in the
humid summer heat imploding
on the dashboard my hand
pressed to the rim of a rolled down
window, the breezes smelling
of camphor trees, staggering wounded
under war paint slashes of sun
Doc's saliva dripping on me
my fingers deep in his fur, I kissed
his head,
his nose;
Dal telling me to sit down straight
and when the Pontiac sedan stopped
he made the long walk to the front door
of the sickness, and pressed the bell
and I, during the half-hour
Doc and I waited
recited *Jack and Jill went up the hill*
or I sang Doc the song *Bill Bailey
won't you please come home*,
or told him Abbot and Costello jokes
Doc and I in the car me with my red purse
swatting at flies or slapping mosquitoes
between my hands

a trick I learned
from my mom. Or maybe
while I tickled Doc's spotted
pink belly, I repeated a speech
I had memorized
from 3 times seeing
My Friend Flicka

At the fountain of Dr. Dry's
Drugstore, a chocolate soda for me
a chicken salad sandwich on toast
for Dal and Doc to split.
The last lap home
an esplanade on Montrose
lined with king palms
that Dale said had marched
from midnight to sunrise just to get there
for us to see; palms they as tall
as the houses that waving fans had entertained
for 30 years front porches with white rattan chairs
a chaise longue, thick flowery cushions
ladies skirts to their ankles
collars hiding their necks,
a Russian wolfhound and a manservant
with a tray of tea and sometimes
a lighted cigarette behind
a *Harpers Bazaar*

These my reflections now
each time I have my stethoscope
around my neck, Dal's gold
fob-watch in my pocket as I walk
the halls of Methodist Hospital
Dal and Doc flooding my mind
as much as when we shared two years
of as-big-as-life Sunday- afternoons.

Trouble was the year before
I had left for boarding school
in Charleston, but first,
Dal and I buried Doc
in the back yard. Doc
loved it there, napping away
the last of his 13 years,
under the pecan tree's
lilac shade.
And then, of course, Dal
in his turn. Doc and Dal,
whom this poem
means to keep alive.

Wanting You: *Eure-et-Loire*

Perhaps it's best not to think of scholars,
or become too involved with one. Thus,
summering in France beside our millrace,
my theory of them came to me in stages,
as peonies go from bulb to bud to bloom,
and detached petals pitch like canoes
over the waterfall
into clear water welling.
In La Perche, alongside the river Eure,
this came to me; and the excesses
of *Le Cour de Louis XV hurt* my head.
by splashing into our millrace's flood
as surely as our willow branches
trail weeping.

Sweetheart, this morning as I was sunning
outside my chamber and heard you scolding
Parisians in peasant dress for interrupting
your studies, by picnicking across the River Eure,
the theory of isolation came to me, mine;
since, as you mowed
our island's lawn, sprinkling
me with grass blades, then crouching near
like a unicorn up from a baron's park,
your bare knees shining, teasing me
about whether flying grass blades
could disturb anyone
then said you had to study
and strode away.

After *un dejeune sur l'herbes*,
when the sun was mimicking
the lipstick of La Pompadour,
causing charcoal in the pit to smoke;

and after my crossing of the wooden bridge
and coming up with the theory of sticker-vines,
pricking my arms and pulling my golden braids,
I spotted you in the hammock, reading
from a small leather copy
of *Les Saisons d'Enfer,*
I moved quickly, *dancing shoes* crushing
September's gilded leaves, snapping dry twigs,-
a duck's green feather between my teeth,
I gave you my red fox stare.
And a twist of my hips,
I made you put down your book.

Memory and Mother Goose
for Margo

Cimarroncita cedars to smell
small fingers to touch the bark
for roughness we jumped
into rapids so cold we screamed,
and Houston girls
saw snow on Baldy's peak
you never queasy
even when a disregarding
horse stepped on your foot,
whinnies of mustangs
lassoes twirling
into the herd one caught
dragged us yards,
we scrambled
to our feet
and set it free

next summer tennis doubles
we won, bravoes from girls 14
some as tough as you and me
sharp shooters lying on our bellies
firing 22s loading bullets
from a lightweight cardboard box
You Hopi chief, I Navajo
fire builder
the Navahos lost so going home
you bought me dinner
on the Pullman we were old enough
to ride at 15 years we talked to boys
in the high school halls
folded our dreams into theirs

two girls teasing, talking fast
boys quiet and scheming

in our 70s I ask you why
you're in room #620
I bend over you your blue eyes
half closed a tube
down your throat
hands 3 times swollen
I remind you that once
we climbed the big guy Baldy
cut our initials
on a flat brown stone. . . .
I hang around while male hands
slide you into an ambulance
as if you were a spray
of winter roses
my car a stoplight behind
turns into hospice
and, my god, trees like cedars
sway under clouds rubbing
together for lightning

so *Hi, diddle diddle*
the Cat and the fiddle
The Cow jumped
over the moon
The little Dog laughed
To see such sport
and the Dish ran Away
with the spoon. I'm home
in candlelight the flame
marching in place
on the sea-quiet color
of a my concrete floor
my glass house
the telephone I listen

to the message then look
through the skylight
at the clicking of polka dot stars
Old Baldy watching
at attention the lightning
ascent of a Hopi chief.

The Last Monarch

I walk beside my man, Finnegan.
We hike down to Mother's
vacation house on the bank
of Sybil Creek. Sharp stones
cause Finnegan to slip.
When he says he is afraid of heights,
I take his hand.
When he weeps, I suggest
a sandy path the Gilas use.
He smiles
then pats his fly
to remind me that he is
expecting a child.

Inside the house, cans pierced
with spent cartridges cover the floor,
and houseflies hang by splintered legs
from window screens, while, in the center
of the kitchen, a chamber-pot
waits in a wooden case.

When Finnegan's hands tremble
on his bowtie, I unfasten
the metal clips. When he asks me
to lift the pot's lid and dust the seat,
I'm glad to do it. On command he pushes.
Using the bowl configuration he makes
with his hands, he drinks those tears, and mine,
then gazes outdoors at a sky changed
from cobalt to black, ticking like clocks
in old-timey depots. When he
requests food, I serve died beef
and cream sauce. When he feels the heat,

his eyes spring like traps
and his skin turns to leather.

At 9 o'clock, as rats take the slope
of the roof
ra-ta-tat-tat
ra-ta-tat-tat
Finnegan gives birth to a son
the size and shape of a caterpillar.
"You may hold him," he says.
Then we, on this asteroid
too small for 3,
watch our boy inch away.

Natural Selection

a shame Evie that at 12 years
you told your friends your dog
descended from a wolf,
lupine stem and placenta
to which puppies attach,
now lying between her legs,
as a redwood root drives down
into a lump of clay
a shame before you got picked off
you thought you wanted
a Darwin's monkey harnessed
to a calliope dancing
on a hangman's rope
your first man a futurist,
though since too shaded
by an avocado tree
of green adolescence
you sent to walk a plank
no needle-eye intrusion
into a sweet vestibule
welcome as vital to a worthy male
as heavy cream to a proper bisque
to serve a king so who was the one
who sacked you
but a blue-eyed Phi Bet
as plug-dangerous as a bull
who hears a heifer's complaint
in a holding pen best to offer your lining
to what he has on this night
of homoerectus amour.

The Lover

he crosses her bedroom
she asleep in a warm pocket
of night flaxen hair spread
on the pillow to stroke
small fist under her chin
one more barefoot step
she's a woman to him
he moves her hand
to touch him
not even a tussle
and she giggling like a baby
as he cleans her up.

outdoors Mama hugs a pine tree
licks rosin and cuts her hand
on the Swiss knife found
in their son's once gorge-tumbled truck
she watches while an owl tears
out the belly of a rodent heart
beating; the wise owl's head quarter turns
to an open window a curtain billowing;
its head jerks back as it catches the scent
of the fitted sheet printed with Cinderellas
each trying on the as yet unidentified shoe.

morning at 5 he leaves
hanging in the barn
a field dressed 12-point buck
he's thinking of the back strap
he'll marinate in wine and give to her;
she'll like it and she'll like him.
next time he'll take her
with him teach her to shoot a bow
and arrow, and at 13, a .38

in the thicket behind the house
a doe's brown eyes ignite,
her strong neck pulling her spotted fawn
close her gritty tongue
licking it behind its ears,
while a rabbit mother on hind legs
waits on the lookout for a raptor,
black-shadowing the pasture,
bounds toward her babies
curled sleeping in a warm hole's
damp sack, worms slithering by
afraid of grass that is too green
and the sun

the child sways neck stretched
from a wire noose fastened to a rafter
the chair she used
turned over to rest
on a broke-back dollhouse
chairs and tables scattered
her setter puppy's head
frowning, rests on crossed paws
small feet swimming in fall's
bronzed breeze, a pair of tennies
and in the barn,
Mama's gun smokes.

The House This October

The house needs help so much it bursts
into tears a jagged gash like lightning
above the front door,
a swatch of paint ripped off
on a sunshine-deal, and yonder chimney
a tower of leaking bricks. See how our tallow trees
turn orange, and sunset fires coral bullets,
though it's not yet six?
See the waxing quarter-moon
over to the left? I'd like to reach up
and hang out the washing, while Pups,
stomach-ached from eating
what Kitty left of a woodpecker,
munches clover.

The house needs a new French door;
that one's flash-rotted from Gulf Coast rain;
the gutter over the kitchen sags
and there's pigeon do thirty times
over on the green striped awning. Do
you see that Jane Warfield's cat is trying
to drink from an overturned birdbath?
But why trespass for so little gain?
Yet I say, Come to me cunning
leonine pastiche. I'll tell you to roll over,
let me pat your velvet belly,
then form a basin of my hands
and let you drink.

What I know is this:
Darrell, you would have cleaned,
striped crisply, painted clearly,
nailed siding in pleats and repaired
the wheelbarrow's broken wheel.

So where are you, your love-woman
here in the kitchen carving a pumpkin
to replicate the disembowelment
of her content? See how she cuts
three-sided eyes, hoping to find
your tall, angular ghost,
wading this morning through mist
rolling through pear trees?
You, who shiver gravely
under serial puddles of rain,
hold a tight-fisted blanket
of stars close under your chin,
while on the family obelisk,
heavy on your chest,
I lean into the winding trail
of bright green moss,
eager to bond with the obduracy
of stone, the muted half of us
I can no longer find.

Baby and Becky

Moon, horns on her adolescence to witness
11:24 Mama wakes her tells her
to take Becky out to pee.
Becky's floppy ears; they take
a gravel park path—above them,
dark April cirrus' clouds lately lengthened
like women's skirts hemmed widely.
Becky squats eyes bulging with happy ease

a truck three men good evening
doors open a boot-heel grinds
a red tip cigarette another thumps
a butt into a sewer grate, he with long hair
a rubber band to hold it
holds her to keep she knows the feel of him
eyes closed he lets go like a slot machine
for Baby to take his profit
and breasts ain't nothing but nubs
the second older by 7 years, third quick
as a cap-pistol
not a fragrant cabbage rose in sight,
nothing but a bud

Becky's ribs cracking
like a pulled wishbone
and the red planet pricks;
tangled tree limbs can't catch their breaths
for howling and Becky's head,
fur knotted rolls like a croquet ball
into a field without wickets
twice the youngest returns;
she drinks that communion three men bathe
at a hydrant, Baby's head half planted
on a redbud's dendrite roots. guests

at mama's party they drink from bottles,
toss beer caps at the Crèche
and into the a red candle,
drowning out the wick
while a 32-year-old man
plays sweetheart to a stray cat
that used to live under the house
Mama's wine sloshing
into a well-made punch
floating with orange slices
once blended for love
and the making of children.

Return to Mayan Hegemony
for Linda Shele

Two refugees from Chichen Itza and Sayil,
ring the door bell, ask to clean my gutters.
I lend them hats, souvenirs from Merida and Tecul.
On my patio tree ferns shake and arc,
laugh like babies if I click my tongue. Sunflowers
and cosmos bow. A gust scatters their seeds,
while lady bugs hang out their domes
and ply an ancient trade.

Above the planted funeral urns of the poodles,
Hector and Rex, tree ferns multiply like rabbits
and a palm tree holds up its skirt to show its leg,
as its core, midwifed by the midday sun,
strains to birth its thirty-first fan.

Sisters clean my gutters. Pods and hulls
tumble to the tympanums of elephant ears;
a flower named Shasta genuflects to show
the matt underside of its spokes.
The older woman wipes sweat from her eyes.
She disgorges trash from a second conduit,
and says to her sister: "We are like these leaves
that future generations will never know or see.
At best, we are crows balanced on telephone wires
that deform our feet."

I open the window. "No es verdad, mujeres.
Since Linda Shele broke the hieroglyphs at Uxmal,
the Pyramid of the Magician functions; Giles
and crickets run free, and jaguars, released
from silver yokes, occupy trailer parks
at Kabah and Becal."
They bag my refuse, bank it at the curb

then catch the Greyhound's favored redeye.
One lives in Chichen Itza,
the other in Sayil.

A Rocky Road

He walks toward the altar,
fists behind his back filled
with Almond Roca; he speaks
dulce vita, tracks sugar
on a silk runner's ruby red.
When Mendelssohn gets his chance
and I take to the aisle,
he calls to me, "Hey, Sugar!"

Alone with the ring bearer, he switches
to divinity, asks me which hand. Does
anyone know why this couple
should not be cooled in an open window?
We leave First Pres under a salvo of M&Ms.
He runs ahead in his cutaway, crowing,
"Snickers by any other name
would taste as . . . ."

Nightfall, he deft as a rabbit
turns me on a greased cookie sheet,
and we melt together. By Michaelmas,
I'm an éclair stuffed with pudding.
When he backs down the driveway, I call,
"Come home early!" Out the car window,
he waves a sticky hand.
"You bet your sweet life!"

Four-thirty, his car pulls into the driveway
slinging gravel. "I'm ready!" he shouts.
"I see that you are."
Next morning, he pops a lifesaver
and calls in sick.

Christmas-ripe, Santa,
though satisfied, hangs another cane
on my peppermint tree. On vacation,
sunrise, twilight, midnight,
he seeds me with marzipan,
shapes his creation me with a buttered finger.
"Good technique," I say.
Come the summer solstice,
a ripening jelly-bean kicks my belly.
As it turns on its side, he offers
a licorice stick: "Suck this."

On election year, we agree to substitute
vanilla for almond, marsala for Harvey's
Bristol Cream. When I come
to room temperature, he breaks me
into sweet pieces. Yet
it wasn't then; it was when
he played hardball
and stirred me too briskly.
The first out of the shoot,
we named Tootsie,
the second Baby Ruth.

One Gerbera

Once a day, a week, I need to see you, gerbera,
a Ming dynasty sunshade that lasts seven days,
green arms rushing to ring the hours
better than hickory,
dickory, or a digital clock.

Yesterday, when you opened out full,
I heard a black bird caw
from a loaded lemon tree,
but it's the scallop-shell birdbath
that gets most of your bloom's mind,

obscured now and then
by a jay couple's wash,
or a dove strolling
from the bath's semi-lune
to the scroll hinge of the axis
it clarifies. You, one golden gerbera
with whom the sun's
red eye flirts,

till you give birth to seeds,
or you dwarf star ripped
from Apollo, cry, oh, God!
as a breeze lifts above your
alluring stem, the perfect circle
of your feathered skirt.

Central Texas 1830

They told us how to do.
We are your angels, they said,
we cared for the conquistadors
of San Antonio as those settlers
broadcast seeds to boost the land's
vigor and worth since charity begins
with extras in filled basket.
On the way to bars and stables,
we rang their bells. Come drought,
floods, twisters, we rang their bells;
they told us how to do.

Shrinking ropes chafed our fingers and ruined
our hands. Blisters covered my Scottish man's arms,
blued his face and he lost one eye. Our rib bones
became catfish spines, and sewing needles
splashed on the Brazos River's shore. You there,
with quilted wings, tried to save our days by leaving
prints of silvered almandine on polished
cedar floors. Shrinking bell ropes
chafed our fingers,
ruined we women's hands.

They told us where the antelopes played,
but our hair pulled out by dust-devils
left scarred pates, and the boys among us,
holding by their nails from cliffs in Bexar County,
were shot through with flintlock arrows.
They told us where rabbits hopped,
ones enslaved by a herd of Jersey bulls.
We complained of tornadoes stealing our roofs
and pulling the nails from our barns.
here a barn, there a barn,
everywhere a barn-barn.

They were our angels.
It would have happened
anyway, they said.

Hurricane Ike

Small Ann to Little Tiffany:
"Today's thunder sounds like Dad
when we pushed Nana's rocking chair
downstairs. See that banana trees rise
like donkey ears to hear; the Chinese elm
has lost its head, and magnolia leaves
make as good a clatter as the Aggie Band,
finishing off. Rain breaks green tomatoes
off their stems, the garden hose slaps
our house's pink brick cheeks,
stars and stripes pop pop pop like cap-guns,
and Spot bounds upstairs to watch
the fuss compound. Look, a pecan tree
has fallen on our phone wires,
and in a minute, we'll get a green nut's call;
the garden hose has slapped our house;
squirrels born last April stumble
into our greenhouse and kick the shins
of Mom's orchids. Lil' Tiffany,
she says God is rocking his own boat,
floors are buckling like frying bacon, and the attic
leaks a nasty yellow stream. Worse still,
Noah and his boy, Shem, are poling a pirogue
up a bayou named Braes.
Small Ann asks Li'l Tiffany
to help her spread a prayer rug,
assume lotus-position,
and become a falling star.
It's the thing to do.
Then tomorrow gather up
the neighbor's broken bones.

Waiting for My Second Child

The dishwasher whirred an interval,
red light flashed like a police car
trailing a truckload of sleaze.
I pressed my cheek to a pink rose
painted on the kitchen counter,
one that, last month, I painted
in the center of each glazed tile.

I had never before created
artwork so tasteless. The only thing close
occurred was when I was pregnant
with my first child, and painted a 1970's
rattan chair the color of a liquid remedy
for the runs; set it in the nursery
and tied to its front legs
blue sateen bows.

After my son's birth,
estrogen levels normal,
I pitched it on the curb,
where 3 chattering kindergarteners,
as fast on it as pigeons to Planters Peanuts,
carted it sedan-chair fashion
to a playhouse; they and I each
with such a precious thing to love.

The Thirteenth Floor

All Souls Day, I sit in a rocking chair,
sunlight and blinds combining to stripe
an ink-blue rug; my forearm shades
my eyes. Dr. Apple says, "I believe
the reason human beings fire guns
at strangers is because they need fathers.
Most of us don't understand ourselves
till a cloud bursts, a cat unlike our own,
enters the glass house of our shower;
the man who assaults us attends
Grace Church, or a picador's lance
bobs in our brown child's neck. "

Her theory and voice decline,
just as the day before the recorded lecture,
*Egyptian Influence on Mesoamerican
Architecture; Is There One?*
declined to my ear, at the same time
that my cocker girl gnawed in twain
my PC's long black cord.

My gaze slides down my white arm
to the watch on my wrist, and then
to the doctor's hands, one of which scrubs,
with four fingers, the opposing palm.
I ask her if, perhaps, her lifeline
is shorter than she thought?
Her hands spring into her jacket pockets.
She reddens, says no; it's that her palm
itches, in the way her father's used to do.

I listen as she relates her history
with a dermatologist, who takes
her money, but offers no useful advice.

It begins to rain, a curtain of water
obscures the stage where Houston's
skyscrapers nap or play. When
Dr. Apple becomes restless, I remove
from a purse, cluttered with scarred pictures
of a once photogenic lover, my Chase Bank
checkbook and write.

Bernini in the Piazza Navona

Gian Lorenzo, scultore,
as we sit in the Piazza Navona,
let me explain myself from *Italian on the Go*.
I came to Rome to meet you, 9 hours
aboard a Boeing 747, breathing fetid air,
eating plastic food, my waste hard
as lava stones.

Signore, Roman master,
one hundred percent Baroque,
I read at home Hibbard's Bernini,
the ecstasy of Saint Teresa of Avila;
an arrow from your grinning angel
directed at her breast, excited carnal dreams
as uplifting as my brother's *Esquire* foldout.

Gianetto,
were you born to scuffed shoes
and drafty mittens, or were your parents
well-heeled? Were you a prodigy,
or a long-time low-achiever
named Late bloomer? Is it true that you,
unlike the saint of Assisi, never slipped
your head into the mouth of the Gubbio wolf
in order to develop
a high sense of prescience?

In room # 4 of the Museo Borghese,
Proserpina's thigh in Pluto's grip seduced me,
thus I came to this fountain to meet you
at the confluence of our shared fixation.
Sit with me at this wobbly table
near the shore of your creation;
slide a couple of napkins

under the delinquent leg as I explain
that my outburst is no metaphor
for male rivers, or the rapture
of an individuated Spanish saint,
but a desire to copulate with genius
touched by grace, enabled
by ecclesiastic reform,
inspired by the ribbon-veins
of Carrara, influenced
by the classicism of Michelangelo,
the beauty of Roman women,
and your need to make a buck.

Requiem

Girls, cover your cornflower eyes;
cotton fields are marching south
and butterflies drown in milkweeds'
sour outpourings. Know that Nanie's
front porch hides its private parts in vines,
withering too quickly; and TEXDOT pulls
her barbed-wire's teeth, leaving
their wiry owners night-crying
in fetid ditches beside FM 456.

Once the grocer in Anahuac asked them
were they twins? They nodded
bird-quick while a watermelon lay on a block of ice
and on Sundays, redwing blackbirds
sat on telephone wires, listening
to a waterfall preach.

You, Grand Parkway, made us climb
too high in Texas; berry pies burned black
issuing purple streams, the midday sun
hung from its broken stem, the barn
echoed small boots climbing to a loft
where four eyes, round to breaking,
watched the muscular mating of cattle
and ignorant August turned the other cheek
to July's fiery slap.

So loosen your holds on berry pails, rake
one last time the shiny buns Skeeter
dropped for crows to peck, and see
that corncobs search among the kernels
for their families. Know that hauler trucks
cross the Parkway's arc where Nanny milked
cows, loaded wood into an iron stove, dished

out buttered oatmeal, poured on heavy cream.
See that workers level her buildings,
pull out by the roots her land's green hair;
and while sobbing cockle-burrs watch,
burn their children one by one.

So wring the neck of the rooster
and hitch the mule's gray bones. They
don't mind. Bend down darkly inside this memoir's
bedroom windows; hear whining grass blades
urge an afterlife to pear trees' fruitless hopes.
Listen carefully to the sprained-fingered breeze,
as it strums a fretting cello's blacktopped field.
Then look behind me as the last cricket plucks
the last pasture's ragweed strings, and tells again
Nanie's stories till the ghosts of the children sleep.

Love

I knew love, I know that. Even on rainy days,
I knew when love was ready to make divinity
that hardens, or a frosting that sticks;
a goshawk to leave a telephone wire in pursuit
of the female that just flew by; a thrush
to swim the yellow grass for more than fun;
a redbird's chip-chip call above Nana's
kitchen door. With you, I knew the best
as I knew a blooded dog by its eyes,
the tilt of its head,
its competent bark –
as I knew a street cat by its belly slink
and that this animal would never play
on a porch floor with a velvet mouse
stuffed with nip. By February,

I knew the grid pattern of waffles,
the nostril-twitching scent of buck wheat,
the translucence of a well made crepe
held before a stained glass window
at the curve of a honeymoon's stairs. For you,
I knew how to refine and become as refined
as it, by moving the mother liquor, surrounding
its hexagonal crystals. I spoke two languages,
had no use for a third. I knew my spirit,
how to achieve for it a dream link with yours. Then
in October, I knew how a baby, stretching its legs
in my body may when things go dull refuse to budge
and must be made to by an O.B.'s deft
hand scraping; I understood that this
same child, making its difficult arrival,
still loved me and that twins two years
later, born easy, loved us both.

I liked words.
When I wanted you, I spoke in similes
to insinuate my body's presence
into your mind. We named each tree
on our property; we healed nefarious growths
on improbable roots. We came to know
that on the limbs of venerable redbuds
purple blossoms grow. We responded
to a lime tree's green shoots with an oration
on the fecundity of its parents. In October,
we talked with leaves, mimicked their flaming
colors, predicted their futures. I knew them
and I know you
as I know the able seed that made me,
and I know that I encouraged the avidity
of yours; the ones
that made our children. I knew our family's security
and route of passage. I knew your strengths
and the absence of them. I approved both conditions.
I quickened to them so never to diminish our pace
as an entity.

In our sun-moon cage 24/7, you completed me
as a growl a lion, and the powder of certain pigeons,
how it galvanizes that bird's ubiquitous coos.
Together, we struggled and played like bear cubs
in Yosemite, chimps in Tanzania; squirrels among
polished sun-winking leaves of magnolias
in our home and down the block.

Not to worry, we intended to make thunder
with our battery-powered wings, and when the hunter
sends bullets, to leave the stage, playing with four hands
The Rhapsody on a Theme by Paganini and closing
Matisse's fuchsia curtain, with our dexterous hands
and the crook of your cane.

Superstition

if you're as free of tides
as bottom fish yet eaten by a shark
disgorged absent a limb
you may not prosper nor escape
being held under the armpit
of a Gulf Coast wave.
If you are led by the spirit,
you will not be subject to the law.
If you were brave before long bows
and the bites of adders
you will soar like a kite
without fear of being jerked
by gusts into leaps
you never practiced
and never meant to take;
you will live to tell your story
to April passerines arriving sunblind
and wingless on the Texas' coast
or to spring days pinked by roses
or frozen in a candytuft of snow;
in fact, you may find in mirrors
a saint's face to place upon your own.
Then under the hum of fan blades
flashing shadows on your bed
or lightning at the windows
or the glow of flashlights
dropped into shallow water
rising to full height
like standing lamps or a reaction
to a Jew's-harp twanging.

If you are standing before bullets
trying your best to blast off
on a childish toy and become Cato's

foolish eagle listening in flight
to the purposeful scuttles of mice
in the grassy field below, perhaps
it's best to beat your wings,
a male condor's prelude to mating,
or a flock of silver-tongued gulls
dipping into well-provisioned wakes
behind shrimp boats, with nothing
to assure their reason than J.M.W. Turner's
bayside sunsets or Sinai's robust dawns
where Moses spoke on yet another occasion
to God. Or like Lucifer at the entrance
of his a cave may have grinned at female spiders
copulating then eating their astonished mates.

Or, reader, see that King Charles'
favorite spaniel lurks inside tufts
of monkey grass beside the curbing
on my street? Judge for yourselves,
for isn't it so that this dog desires to crush
the bones of Chicken Little,
rip Thunderhead's pasterns before he can kick
then sit laughing,
recalling Dr. Faustus' frolic
before his cruel extinction since the devil
abides behind any face? Or would you,
after all I've said, still fear you might hire
an NFL center (You know that Hercules)
to patrol the limits of your land,
answer to your children's softest cries,
and install an alarm system
and electric gates?

Dad and the Kingfisher

the house on the hill bought
for their retirement
Mom and Dad's place
two acres of ground,
a swimming pool
at the brink of a cliff
months of skinny-dips
flamingo swatches of sunset
winding up and winding down
the hill's wooded spools to thread
each July sisters brothers grill
supper on the terrace till dark
13 grandchildren for a month
in summer, 6 young adults
sitting at the breakfast table till 9
chewing eggs, bacon, oatmeal
and brown sugar slipping
down throats, processing
but not always swallowing
Ronald Reagan; making fun
of society photos, rich people
thinking they are better than?

ten years of it then in '82,
Dad breaks his heart and Mom's
with margaritas, enchiladas, salty chips,
then she standing by the wall-sized window
eyes misty as London mornings;
half closed, she squints at Austin town,
and a river named Colorado
while on the 4th, fireworks hurt her ears
she for 3 years 24/7 keeps
her pistol by her side cocked to kill

we move her to a townhouse
on Bull Creek, she alone,
even 2 grandchildren married
into busy homes dotting San Antonio
and the West Coast one of the girls
a military historian at West Point
otherwise doctor lawyer merchant
chief cowboy sailor tinker tailor

Four o'clock,
on a January afternoon
sunny as a kids camp in Kerrville
Mom reaches out from her balcony
to stroke a kingfisher
up from the creek wings feathered
emerald yellow weskit
his diving for her
soaring to show he can
perched on the railing he shakes
his tail and struts
he in love again
her eyes green
a perfect match for him
and thinks of babies.

The French Lover

The willow leaves are weeping
as they do and I wait for you
in coral silk, the color of the tassels
on our curtain pulls and of the sun
each time it pleased it to set.
Come to me if you want to live again
in this rural setting; eat the hare
and break the melon; kiss my hand,
join our forces, share both picnic blanket;
the king of the goose-down bed and a cave
filled with wines from Vosne Romanee
and Beaune.

Send word if you'll need on arrival
a hunting horse, hard copies of Proust,
Stendhal,
and Louis XIV's tricky satirist
Jean Baptiste Poquel Moliere
read comfy in your wicker chaise,
words lit by the polished steel lamp
you said looked like a grasshopper
set to steal Pere Lapin's ripe corn.

Let me know when you are here
by pulling hard on the bell rope out front.
Come to me if you want to live again
in this rural setting. Send word by a
peripatetic fox pin a note to its ruff,
arrange for tinders to spark
in its charcoal eyes.
You may be thinking what will she want with me
at our mill west of Chartres, she overburdened
as she thinks she is, with weight gain, crow's feet,
and eyes dulled by the skies that only sing

in summer.
But I tell you,
the willow branches
still swim boldly beside this millrace,
and red globe-like dahlias still bloom
behind the bedroom's
double doors. In all these years
of the river's flowing
past La Loupe and Belomert,
their flowers have neither lost
their faces' sun-fist magenta
nor their wish to spend the summer
with our spirits here in this house,
this erstwhile Eden,
this cool gray cave.

King Lion II

threw down his French history book,
ran through our garden, "*Jonche de fleurs
et de rameaux.*"
He cracked his head on the visibility of beams,
slashed a hind leg on a meat hook. He tumbled
laughing like a night animal up from the woods,
then sprawled up a bank. Cold and wet
he fell on me, as before, his calling me
by his pet name
for female swallow birds. He shook
our bouquet of iron flowers off its base,
kicked it's petals. Sore of foot, he hopped upstairs,
caught me by the waist beside a trundle bed.

    "Ahi!"
    "Ahi!"

King Lion II
ran through Dada's vineyard,
with me on his mind. Grabbing his mane,
I held him from my face. He lost that hair;
he trembled, panted under bruised leaves,
his paw resting on my chest. He glanced up
at a moonstruck owl, shared with it a smile,
King Lion proud of his success.

    "Ahi!"
    "Ahi!"

That's the way
it was at the millhouse's entrance,
75 minutes southwest of Paris.
Was that *le Grand Siècle*
or *L 'Age Dore*? I examined my tongue.

Was it I who had licked the bronze
from the drawer-pull
of *Chere Commode*?
Had the Sun King
commissioned
Monsieur A. C. Bouille
to make furniture for us?
Reader, awake, arise and look
King Lion II thinks
he's given me twin cubs.
See how boldly he wakes from sleep?

William

You and I live in a house
on easy street. Dad works downtown,
Mom paints pictures of fishing boats,
fruit bowls, and mountains in Alpine.
Our furniture is hand-me-downs and Mission,
our family made to last. For the war effort
we own a B-sticker Buick. You marry
your high school quarterback William.
For Christmas he's in the Ardennes,
and your belly's a balloon.

We have an attic room to read in,
a camphor tree to climb, a wading pool
to pretend is as fun as the closed public pool.
America has croquet, Jack Benny, Dennis Day,
and Rochester. Our yard is sky high and wide
enough for kickball, but Roosevelt
and Mickey Mouse give the boys sugar, meat,
and Mary Janes. Till all we are is Pearl Harbor
and Ernie Pyle's Bulge, your hair
sun-bleached corn-silk and lemon,
lips Revlon Cherry.

So why a telegram sticking out of your diary,
idle yellow tongue that it is, typed letters
dark as last night to melt your sugar heart
as a blue gas pilot-light
softens honey? The war ends.
your last letter returned:
Dear William . . . .

January 4th, with your blue-green,
gold-star stare, you give birth to a boy
among the dolls we hug to death

for crying. A two-faced sunset
sits on the kitchen table; then Billy,
after shaking hard his clown-face rattle,
laughs and throws it at our father, whom
for all the world he thinks is his.

Spindle Piece

Andre Segovia, we want to show you
our Henry Moore. He told us where to place it;
he said, "On the 31st of October, in the year 1979,
on the night that Houston honors all souls,
with The Moonlight Bicycle Ramble,
my sculpture will be here placed."

I replied, "On Halloween Day, the faithful
will celebrate bronze, believers hold hands
and embrace. Houston cyclists,
many of them native sons, will make 20 miles
seem like one. When we are ready, I'll give
you a side glance and say, 'Maestro Segovia,
I was born in Houston
and you in Valladolid, but tonight
we need something British.

On this clay knoll of Allen Parkway,
beside Buffalo Bayou's tinctured banks,
we have agreed to place Henry Moore's
Spindle Piece, and while 50,000
bicycle spokes blink at the moon, you will sit
on a folding canvas director's chair and play
Frederick Handel
Thomas Tallies,
Benjamin Britten,
and Ralph Vaughan Williams.
for Henry Moore.'"

Sharp Edges

You say that pruning is your gift,
whacking off with shears your occupation.
You cover our lawn with stems wilting
while your cut branches block the bayou;
spoil the turtles' homes, and limit places
for the newts to sun.

You say new shoots
will be here before the vacation
you refuse to take. You ask me what I want,
but when I answer, you make me
share my complaints
with your Mama Grotesque.

I want a forest, a grove in lockstep,
but Mama G. tells me to leave this to you,
who have an imagination to astonish
the folklorists. And haven't I seen you turn
our thicket of yellow roses
into a gaggle of geese;
made a copse of privet into a train of boxcars;
Barbados cherries into dancing bears;
magnolia trees into flag poles; and how about
the fig-ivy of a stallion, chasing to pierce
each one of a frightened trio of mares?

When Mama G asks did I think men
like you grow on trees, I nod,
then leave her home
with our weeping son,
his hair cut short,
his pants above his knees,
his pink receiving-blanket
now so short it belies its name.

Then Mama G, gathering him up
offers a bone dry breast,
and says to me: "His best idea is pruning
and cutting you off."

Then baby and I, ride a Farris wheel,
flying by whatever pieces
you've left of Pisces,
Andromeda, Stella
and a full moon,
which during our courtship,
you repeatedly claimed to love.

The French Hare

Paris.
You come through the apartment's
double doors,
in your arms
our cat slipped
from the balcony three floors up,
our son Sam beside you, trying to touch.
I look close; not Kitty,
but a hare you say killed
near Rimbaud's Charleville
by a colleague at work.

Head, paws, ears, bowels
down the garbage chute,
then we skin it to red flesh
three days marinating in onions
bay leaves and red wine.
And we feast.

Then you, Kitty, eyes shot through
with arrows begging, Sam
gives you part of a leg
you hold between your paws,
hunch your shoulders, needle teeth,
one eye shut, as your counterfeit
lion head turns to crush the bone.

French Landscapes

It's colder here than in Paris or Rouen
our car lights scratch the black of night's back
bien capable, and dims the daylight
out of a once bruised dirty fat-ass moon.
Quinze juillet, rabbits run the roads. Pay attention.

Here in *La Perche*, chestnut trees
don't move and plane trees
are not endangered. The Eure
stays high in its banks and crimson
dahlias have advised us
of their willingness to become
photographs for our bedroom's walls.

I ask you, "Where are you going, honey,
you like a sunset painted Rousseau tiger,
ambling among the river's wet reeds?
Or where are you coming from, hun?"
I can scarcely hear your answer,
swirling as I am in Van Gogh's summer colors
as they call to me from noontime
when pea fields burned ragged
by the sun drift into our unspoken
pride in lassitude.

In this exhaustive year of agriculture
let's visit the battle fields of Clovis,
Charlemagne, and Le Marechale Ney.
Let's not stand here trying to coo like doves,
our knees cut off, first in wheat,
now in deep water rising
a confining dam breeding a suit
of green moss.
For where in this humid portion

of soft air goes the scarlet breath
of our hearts, or sticky stems of strawberries?
They go to us and we blend
with them into crème fraiche
or a lemony sauce of *beurre blanche*.

Have you finished fishing for *tanches*
and *truites*? Then help me taste
this country, swallow it whole.
Put your hands on my waist,
your arms around parts of me you prefer. For
here we are, feet in the water,
breaths giving a tip
to a hard-working yellow breeze.
Let's take a spin in the rowboat;
go where no one will see us
so awkward, playing under the vault of a bridge
the top of it sheltered by a sun-feasted
willow branch, mouth to mouth,
stern to stern; hidden like young foxes
and almost as quiet.

Mount Sinai

You turn your body to me,
with the muscularity of a seal
in a jump. Neither of us has power or wish
to change;
we are young
and aware of the need
we'll have to nurture when the sun sets
how we'll circle one another touching;
smile and talk, take audible breaths,
knowing
where we are going and why.

On honeymoon, you squeeze my hand
while a driver holds the bridle
of a well-fed camel. Together, we rock
to the summit of Mount Sinai. Soon
Moses' tablet of laws settles in, stars jerk above us,
as if standing on hot coals, and the dawn,
like a red bird preening, dons for the good battle
its cape marinated in essence and blood
from a carrion's groin.

Leaving Cairo, in a 747,
seats over the wings,
we sleep, then watch *High Noon*.
Houston, we enter our home
on Milford Street,
happy as little kids, playing
in a public swimming pool,
memories of shelf-breasted grandmothers
keeping watch.

www.ingramcontent.com/pod-product-compliance
Lightning Source LLC
Chambersburg PA
CBHW020943090426
42736CB00010B/1236